Origami for Mindfulness

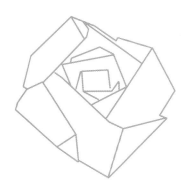

Origami for Mindfulness

COLOR and FOLD your way to inner peace
with these 35 calming projects

Comes with 61 *origami* paper sheets—including 30 to color in

MARI ONO

CICO BOOKS

LONDON NEW YORK

Published in 2016 by CICO Books
An imprint of Ryland Peters & Small Ltd
20–21 Jockey's Fields   341 E 116th St
London WC1R 4BW   New York, NY 10029

www.rylandpeters.com

10 9 8 7 6 5 4 3

Text © Mari Ono 2016
Design, illustration, and photography
© CICO Books 2016

A CIP catalog record for this book is available from the
Library of Congress and the British Library.

ISBN: 978 1 78249 405 8

Printed in China

Editor: Robin Gurdon
Designer: Emily Breen
Photographer: Geoff Dann
Paper illustrator: Takumasa Ono
Stylist: Nel Haynes

Art director: Sally Powell
Production manager: Gordana Simakovic
Publishing manager: Penny Craig
Publisher: Cindy Richards

Contents

Origami and Japanese People

WHY *ORIGAMI* CULTURE WAS CREATED IN JAPAN

The basic tenets of Japanese culture have been driven by a combination of factors unique to the country: long-term settled stability, the importance of following the changing seasons, and the beauty of straight lines, squares, and rectangles, reflected in the patterns of the rice fields that Japanese people are used to seeing everywhere. The straight lines are also reflected in the Japanese cedars and cypresses that grow straight up into the sky and are the essential materials for Japanese architecture—which, like much of Japanese culture, is characterized by straight lines and squares.

THE CULTURE OF FOLDING AND THE CULTURE OF ORIENTATION OF FACING INWARD

Until the beginning of the 20th century, the precision that runs through so much of Japanese culture was epitomized by the way the people folded and stored their bedding neatly every day. The Japanese word for "fold" is the same as the word for "tidy up" and the same practice also applied to clothing—put away almost ritualistically in a chest of drawers—and the *tatami* mat found in almost every Japanese room.

The importance of tidiness to Japanese heritage was most probably born from the diligence of rice farmers. Very early in prehistory it was discovered that rice grew best in a continual cycle of cultivation, allowing famers to settle down in one place long before the more nomadic peoples of China and Europe, where the farmers of sheep, cows, and camels continuously followed their herds from pasture to pasture.

There is a phrase—*issho kenmei*—which means doing things with utmost effort, literally *issho*, meaning "one place," and *kenmei*, meaning "devoting one's life to accomplish something." The Japanese were always living by facing inward into their community, allowing them to use their limited natural resources effectively while creating a wrapping culture which prized the virtue of modesty.

OMOTENASHI, THE JAPANESE SPIRIT OF HOSPITALITY, AND ORIGAMI

The culture of *omotenashi* (the Japanese spirit of hospitality) has been attracting worldwide attention in recent years. The wrapping culture, which is the immediate origin of *origami*, was created from the mind of this *omotenashi*. Giving a gift or money to someone after wrapping it nicely using beautiful paper or cloth is one of the Japanese people's customs and it is still upheld in modern times. For example, most people in Japan don't rip the wrapping paper off a gift but unwrap it carefully so that it is not damaged. They then don't throw it away in a bin, but fold it neatly and keep it for another time. This expresses their sincere feeling for the gift-giver. Also, at the same time of showing the mind of *omotenashi*, it relects the ideal Japanese lifestyle of simplicity and frugality.

INTRODUCTION OF PAPER AND DEVELOPMENT OF DURABLE JAPANESE PAPER

Japanese paper is thin, durable, and difficult to tear. Its most obvious and important use has always been for writing. However, responding to the various demands of paper use, it began to be used in the living environment, for example for *fusuma* (Japanese sliding doors) and *byoubu* (Japanese folding screens), and then developed into *shouji* (wooden sliding doors covered with translucent paper), *chouchin* (Japanese lanterns), *andon* (fixed paper-enclosed lanterns), fans and folding fans, and paper clothes. In such a trend, the creation of the paper for gift wrappings and paper dolls used in purification rites became quite varied as well. Paper amulets and incense wrapping, which are thought of as the root of *origami*, were also created in this trend for varying paper usage according to the people's demand.

The Birth of *Origami*

The exact origin of *origami*, though, is not clear. It is said that one of its earliest instances was the decorative paperwork used in the Shinto ceremonies. Paper being a valuable commodity, it was regarded as divine and nobles would exchange letters or gifts attached with a cut paper now known as a *noshi*. In samurai society, traces of *origami* could be seen in their special style of wrapping developed during the Muromachi Period (1338—1573). But what is quite clear is that in the Edo Period, when paper production increased massively, it became widely popular among ordinary townspeople. *Origami* cranes and various types of boat designs became popular as decorations on clothing, and are depicted in Ukiyoe wood prints. The world's oldest paper-folding text book, *Hiden Senbazuru Orikata* (The Secret of One Thousand *Origami* Cranes), published in 1797, describes how to create many cranes connected together. This was followed by *Kayaragusa* (1845), which provides a comprehensive collection of *origami* models. Recreational *origami* developed as an amusement and method of decoration throughout society.

WASHI JOINS THE WORLD

After a long period of seclusion from the world, Japan relaxed her isolation in 1853. In 1873, at the Vienna World Exposition, Western people were surprised to see various commodities made of paper, such as parasols, rain umbrellas, folding fans, and fabrics made from shifu, which were exhibited by Japan. For Westerners, paper was merely a medium for writing, painting, and printing. Washi's thin and soft but resilient characteristics enabled the Japanese to use it in various ways, from daily necessities to recreational and artistic uses. Washi is now actively used in various categories of work: arts, crafts, bookbinding, graphic design, and interior design to name a few. *Origami* is not only a popular activity among children but it has become a hobby for adults. It is used for recreational purposes, but there are now many *origami* creators whose works have even reached the level of fine art.

At a similar time, near the start of the Meiji era, *origami* was introduced into kindergarten education, and at the elementary schools, students started learning *origami* in their class for arts and crafts, so it became more popular until nowadays *origami* has spread throughout the world.

Origami for Therapy

EFFECTIVE USE OF *ORIGAMI*

Many people consider *origami* to be just a children's play activity. However, in recent years, a variety of effective uses have been revealed. Similar to the "adult coloring books for relaxation" we can get unexpected benefits that go beyond the field of play. It has quite attractive effects on our body such as brain activation and can have a therapeutic effect which can heal the mind. What are these therapeutic effects specifically?

Releasing stress

Through the process of folding a piece of paper one fold at a time, *origami* creates any variety of shapes, from animals and flowers to geometric forms. When we are working to create the models, we sometimes forget the time and become really enthralled in the activity. Such time allows us to free our mind from worldly thoughts and this has the effect of releasing stress. *Origami* for adults is an easy way of releasing stress which doesn't require any tools, can be done anywhere, and which doesn't cost much at all.

Relaxation effect

Most adults have less time to be relaxed as they are always busy paying attention to many things. But *origami* can bring them such a relaxing time. In choosing paper in a favorite color and pattern, then working it fold by fold, this work can relax away tension.

Cerebral activation by *origami*

There are many nerves in the tips of the fingers. Because the nerves are linked to our brain, moving the fingers of both hands is a great way of training our cerebrum. Using the tips of our fingers by folding *origami* paper allows us to activate the brain and it is one of the most suitable recreational activities to allow us to stay young and live longer.

As a result of an investigation by Gakken Institute in Japan, it was found that the level of brain activation by the movement of our fingertips when folding *origami* paper is quite high. It is even much higher than when doing puzzles and playing chess, activities for which we also use our fingers. According to the investigation, the third most effective was the *kendama* (a traditional Japanese skill toy), the second most effective was a math puzzle, and the most effective was *origami*. They found that the work of folding *origami* paper increased the volume of blood flow in the brain the most. It is also known that it is effective for the prevention of dementia in the field of preventive medicine.

Anti-aging effect

Nowadays, at hospitals and care centers all over Japan, *origami* has been introduced into the care programs for the patients' cerebral activation and well-being. This is because when they are folding *origami* paper, the brain activation mode becomes high and when they are creating something, the concentration mode becomes high.

In particular, this type of work, with which they can visually enjoy a variety of colors and create the cranes, airplanes, and flowers while moving their fingertips, requires them to remember the process of folding. The use of a

variety of brain functions to check the balance at each stage of the folding process or choosing a good color to present the sense of seasons can be very effective for dementia prevention.

Also, it is possible to change the level of difficulty of the work according to the level of fingertip movement. Furthermore, at home or at the care centers, people can discuss the works which they have created with family members or friends, and show the works they have made to each other etc, and this leads to an increase in communication.

Origami increases our creativity and joy

The usage range of *origami* doesn't finish when we complete a work but it also extends to arranging a place to put it and imagining and designing how we can finish the final work. Expanding our creativity allows us to acquire a sense of accomplishment and satisfaction, and the joy makes our heart broader and richer. In fact, people who are teaching at an *origami* workshop say that looking at the completed works is a moment of bliss.

I have also received a variety of messages from others such as "I didn't know how mindful the *origami* was," "*Origami* brought me happiness," "So much fun," "I feel brighter," "It makes me excited," "I can spend a day having fun," "I can get motivated," and "I stopped feeling depressed" etc. We can see that it has a very good effect on our mental health. Now you, too, can train your brain with *origami* and have fun.

COLOR THERAPY

This book also comes with a selection of papers to color in. Like *origami*, the process of coloring is a meditative one that reduces stress and enables you to find inner calm. It encourages you to live in the moment and the concentration and repetition of coloring helps you to tune out the stresses of everyday living. You can use the photographs as a guide for coloring the papers or create your own unique designs.

Key to Symbols

Throughout the projects you will notice arrows on some of the step-by-step images. These are useful visual instructions to help you make each model. Below is a key to the meaning for each of these arrows:

FOLDING DIRECTION
Fold the entire paper over in this direction

OPEN OUT
Open out and refold the paper over in the direction shown

TURN OVER
Turn the paper over.

MAKE A CREASE
Fold the paper over in the direction of the arrow, then open it out again.

ROTATE
Spin the paper according to the number of degrees specified in the step instructions.

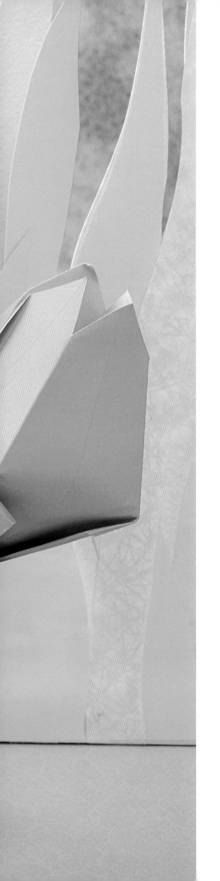

CHAPTER 1

LOVE & HOPE

Ippitsusenn
Heart Message Card

Adding just a few words to a handmade *origami* message card can make a very nice surprise for a close friend. Making one is actually very simple so practice and then create your own message cards using any beautiful paper.

You will need:
1 sheet of 6in (15cm) *origami* paper (if you are using coloring paper, color it in before you start folding)
Scissors

Difficulty rating: ✳ ✳ ✳

1 Fold the paper in half lengthwise to make a crease, then use a pair of scissors to cut the paper in half along the crease.

2 Take one of the pieces and fold it in half from bottom to top to make a crease and open out.

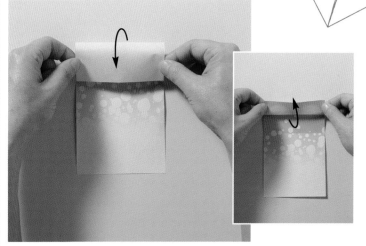

3 Fold the top edge down to the central crease and make a new crease, then fold the edge back to what is now the top of the object.

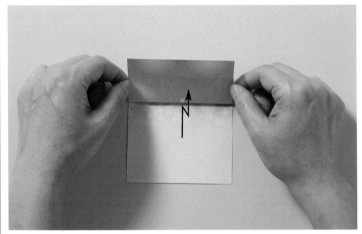

4 Now fold the flaps of paper over themselves in order to form a fourth crease.

5 Open out the crease just made and the adjoining one, then lift the top of the paper and fold it back downward, reversing the direction of the last crease made in the previous step as shown.

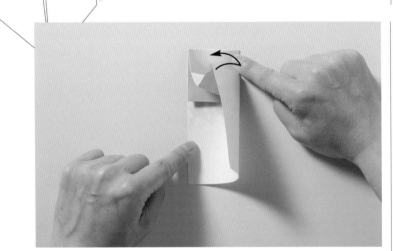

6 Fold the paper in half lengthwise, checking the folds are shown in the photograph, pressing a new crease just at the top of the object over the folded part of the paper.

7 Open out the crease and fold both edges into the center, again making new creases just over the folded parts of the paper.

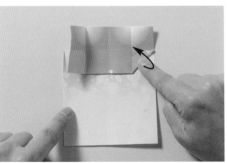

8 Open out again and fold up the lower corners of folded paper diagonally as shown here.

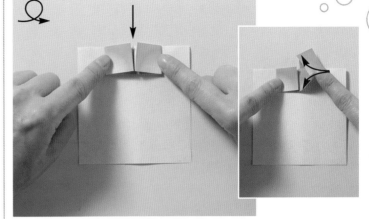

9 Open up the sides and refold the flaps, turning the sides into the middle and creating new triangular folds.

10 Turn the paper over and fold the protruding squares of paper back over the main part of the paper. Next fold the upper flaps of these squares back up, creating a new diagonal edge.

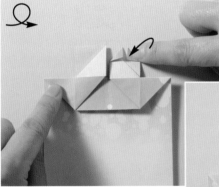

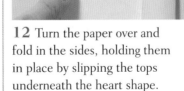

11 Turn the paper back over and fold in the corners of the protruding squares as well as the new tips these folds create.

12 Turn the paper over and fold in the sides, holding them in place by slipping the tops underneath the heart shape.

Sakura
Cherry Blossom

This design can not only be used as a coaster or small plate for candy, but also as an appliqué or wall decoration if made from card rather than paper. Make other flowers—for example a plum-blossom—by cutting different petal shapes in the final step.

You will need:

1 sheet of 6in (15cm) *origami* paper (if you are using coloring paper, color it in before you start folding)
Scissors

Difficulty rating: ✳ ✳ ✳

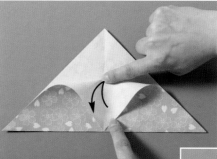

1 With colored side down, fold the paper in half from corner to corner, then open out and repeat, then fold down one flap from the top to the bottom edge and make the new crease just in the center. Release it and fold down the top tip to the mark you just made.

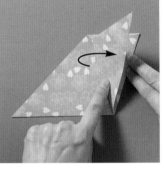

2 Fold over the right-hand side of the paper, making a crease line from the right-hand end of the top horizontal crease to the middle of the bottom edge. Next fold the tip back so that the lower edge runs along the diagonal edge of the object.

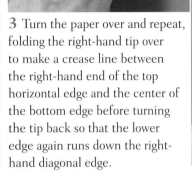

3 Turn the paper over and repeat, folding the right-hand tip over to make a crease line between the right-hand end of the top horizontal edge and the center of the bottom edge before turning the tip back so that the lower edge again runs down the right-hand diagonal edge.

4 To finish, cut out the petal shape as shown and open out the paper.

Tsuru
Crane

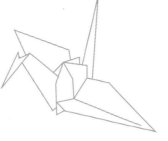

The most traditional and popular *origami* model of all, the crane is known as a symbol of long life and peace. Make a *senbazuru*—a bunch of one thousand *origami* cranes threaded on a string—as a token for a sick person in a hospital.

You will need:
1 sheet of 6in (15cm) *origami* paper (if you are using coloring paper, color it in before you start folding)

Difficulty rating: ✳ ✳ ✳

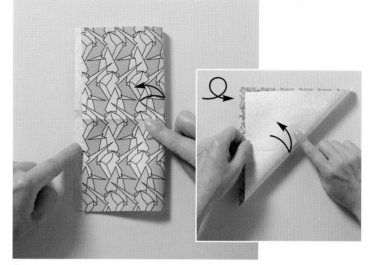

1 Begin by folding the paper into a diamond shape. With the colored side down, fold the sheet from side to side both ways, opening out each time, then turn it over and fold it from corner to corner both ways, again opening it out each time.

2 Now lift the paper off the table and use the creases to fold it into a diamond shape.

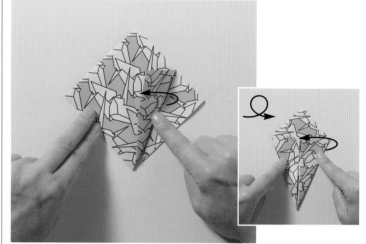

3 Fold in the folded sides of the upper flaps so that they meet along the center line, then turn the paper over and repeat on the other side.

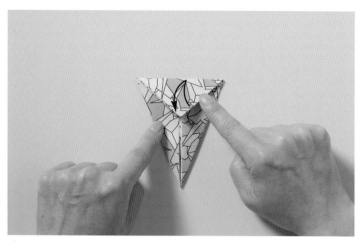

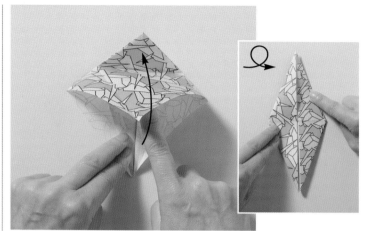

4 Fold down the top point between the outer points to make a crease before releasing it.

5 Open out the upper flaps, then turn up the top sheet of paper, turning it back to the top while refolding the sides into a long diamond. Turn the paper over and repeat on the other side. You will end up with a long diamond shape.

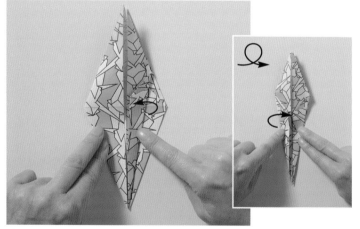

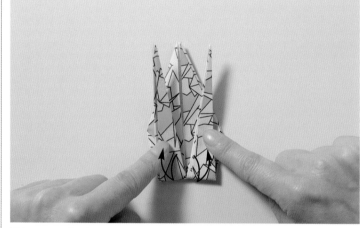

6 Fold in the lower edges of the diamond so that they meet along the center line. Again, turn the object over and repeat on the other side.

7 Turn up both long points, making horizontal creases at the point they join the main body of the model, then release.

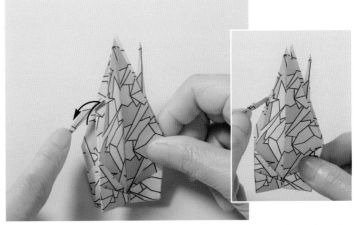

8 Lift up the object and open out one side, folding the long point up, using the crease just made. Close up the side again, enclosing the long point inside it. Repeat on the other side.

9 To form the bird's head, fold down the tip of one side and make a diagonal crease, then gently open up the flap and refold the tip inside it, reversing the direction of the creases where necessary.

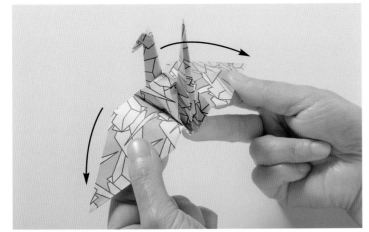

10 To finish, gently pull the wings down and outward while pressing up from underneath to form the shape of the crane's body.

Kikyo
Balloon Flower

In *hanakotoba*, the Japanese language of flowers, the *kikyo* signifies everlasting love. Take care when making the early creases on this model: if they are not pressed strongly enough, the final result will never be as beautiful as you would like.

You will need:

1 sheet of 6in (15cm) *origami* paper (if you are using coloring paper, color it in before you start folding)
Pencil or pen

Difficulty rating: ✳ ✳ ✳

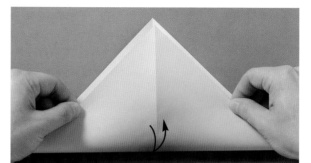

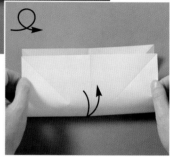

1 This model starts with the paper folded into a triangle so, starting with the colored side down, fold the sheet in half from corner to corner, opening out each time, then turn it over and fold it from side to side both ways, again opening out each time.

2 Lift the piece of paper off the table and use the creases to form it into a triangle.

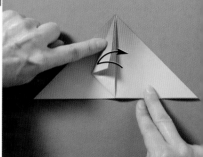

3 The triangle has four flaps and the aim of the next four steps is to fold each of these flaps into a diamond shape. Start by folding the upper flap from the left-hand point so that the bottom edge runs along the central crease. Turn the upper edge of this flap into the center to form a crease.

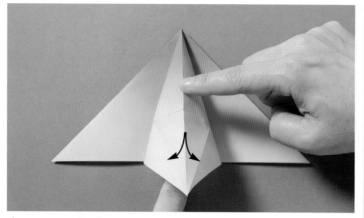

4 Open out the folds just made and flatten the flap, centering it down the middle of the paper.

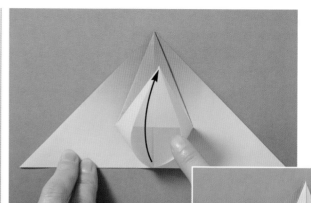

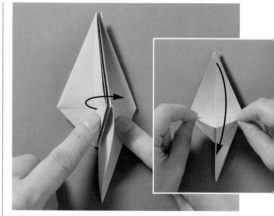

5 Fold the bottom tip up to the top of the paper and flatten it so that it forms a diamond shape. Turn over the paper and repeat Steps 3 to 5.

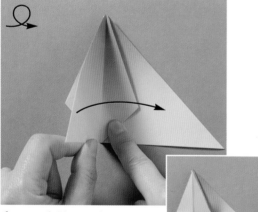

6 Next, fold over the inner flap to the right before lifting the left-hand flap, as shown. Repeat Steps 3 to 5 again on the third large flap to form a third diamond shape.

7 Turn the model back over, fold over the small inner flap, and repeat Steps 3 to 5 on the final large flap. Once this last flap is folded into a diamond shape, fold the upper flap down to the bottom.

8 Fold two flaps from the left over to the right, then fold down the flap revealed, from the top to the bottom. Next turn the model over and repeat so that all four flaps are pointing to the bottom.

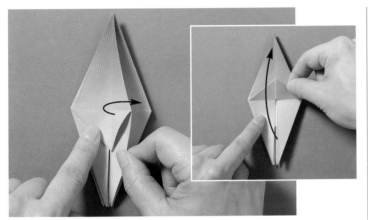

9 Fold over one flap to reveal the small flap inside, then turn it to face upward. Go around the model, finding all the other small flaps and turning them upward.

10 Lift the model off the table and begin to form the shape of the flower. Insert a finger into the model to create the shape of the petals, pushing out the creases to hold them in place.

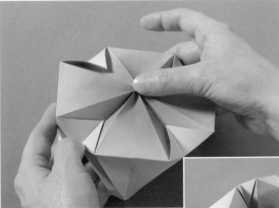

11 Gently use your thumb to push the center point back down inside the model to form a conical shape while retaining the structure of the petals.

12 To finish, roll the petal tips around a pencil or pen to give them the curved shape of the *kikyo*.

Cho Butterfly

The paper butterfly is very easy to make so create a lot of them in different sizes and papers to decorate your room. The curve of the body can be made naturally due to the elasticity of the paper, so make sure not to make any unnecessary creases.

You will need:
1 sheet of 6in (15cm) *origami* paper (if you are using coloring paper, color it in before you start folding)
Scissors

Difficulty rating: ✳ ✳ ✳

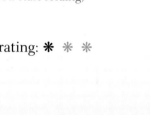
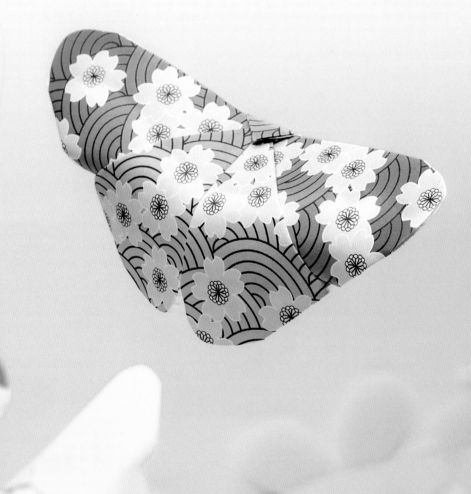

1 With the colored side down, fold the paper in half from corner to corner both ways, opening out each time, then turn the paper over and fold in half from side to side both ways, again opening out each time. Pick up the sheet and fold it into a triangle using the creases just made. Next fold the paper in half from side to side.

2 Use the scissors to cut a curve around one side point, then open out the paper.

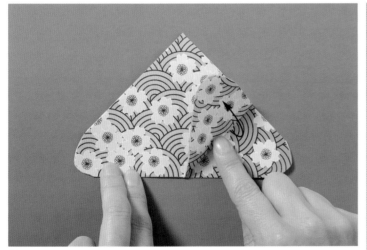

3 Fold the upper flaps on both sides so that the bottom edges meet along the vertical center line.

4 Turn the paper over and fold down the top point so that the tip lies just below the paper's bottom edge; the rounded wings will lift slightly from the table. To finish, tuck the tip underneath the edge and press it into place.

Fusenbako
Balloon Box

Easy to make using a big piece of paper such as wrapping paper, the *fusenbako* can be a useful container for items of all shapes and sizes. Make a variety of boxes, adjusting the size of the top opening part when making them.

You will need:
1 sheet of 6in (15cm) *origami* paper (if you are using coloring paper, color it in before you start folding)

Difficulty rating: ✳ ✳ ✳

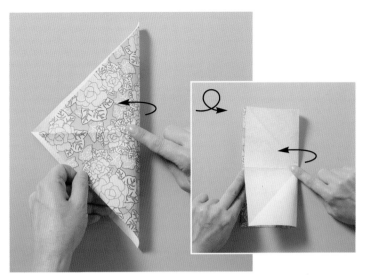

1 With the colored side down, fold the paper in half from corner to corner both ways, opening out each time, then turn the paper over and fold in half from side to side both ways, again opening out each time.

2 Next pick up the sheet and fold it into a triangle using the creases just made.

3 Turn down the top point at a point ½in (1cm) from the tip and pinch the edges to make horizontal marks. Release and fold up the upper flaps so that the corners meet the marks just made. Now fold in the outer corners of these flaps to the vertical edges on each side.

4 Turn the paper over and repeat the previous step on the other side.

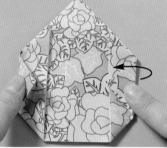

5 Fold the top of the right flap down over the diagonal edge to make a crease and then release before folding down the top point to make a horizontal crease, ensuring that the outer edge of the flap now runs along the same diagonal edge. Repeat with the left flap.

6 Carefully open up the top pocket on each side and tuck in the point folded in the previous step. Repeat with both flaps on the other side.

7 Fold down the top point to make a horizontal crease and release.

8 Lift the paper off the table and carefully start to open it out by placing one or two fingers inside the opening.

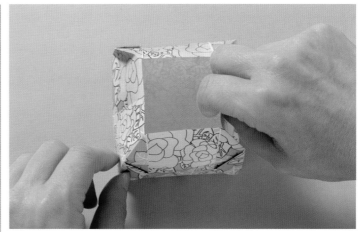

9 Straighten all the edges and press the creases into place to finalize the shape of the box.

Tulip
Tulip

Regarded as a confession of love in the *hanakotoba* (the language of flowers) in Japan, the tulip is a pretty flower that also has a strength which helps signal the arrival of spring.

You will need:
1 sheet of 6in (15cm) *origami* paper (if you are using coloring paper, color it in before you start folding)
Cutting mat, craft knife, and metal rule
Scissors

Difficulty rating: ✳ ✳ ✳

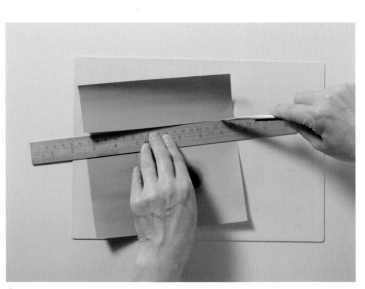

1 Using a cutting mat, craft knife, and metal rule cut across the width of the paper along the edge of the square design, then turn the paper over and repeat. Retain the long edge and discard the short one.

2 With the colored side down, fold the paper in half from side to side both ways, opening out each time, then turn the paper over and fold in half from corner to corner both ways, again opening out each time. Pick up the sheet and fold it into a square using the creases just made.

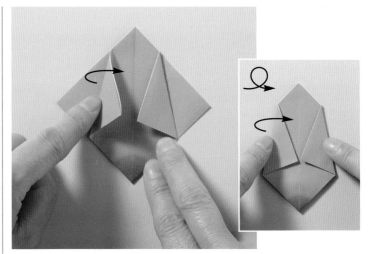

3 Fold in the outer corners of the upper flaps at an angle equal to each other, leaving diagonal edges, and then turn the paper over and repeat.

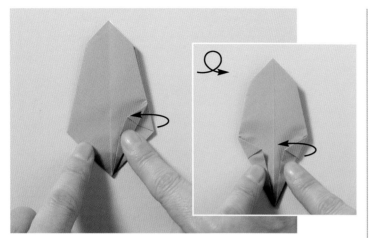

4 Turn over the left-hand flap and fold the bottom right edge in half way to the center line. Repeat on the left, then turn the paper over and repeat the step on the other side.

5 Carefully use the scissors to cut off the bottom tip about $\frac{1}{8}$in (3mm) from the end.

6 Gently use a finger to open out the tulip, pressing the creases flat to create the bulb shape.

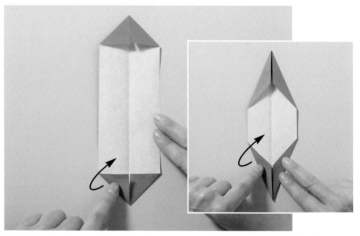

7 Take the longer length of green paper and, colored side down, fold it in half lengthwise to make a crease, then open it out again and fold in the corners so that the ones from each end meet on the center line. Next fold over the diagonal edges so that they also meet on the center line.

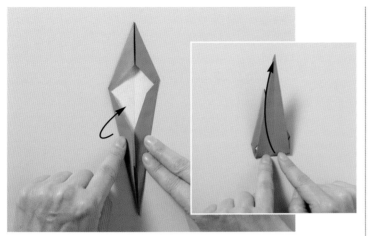

8 Fold in the lower diagonal edges in the same way, then turn up the bottom tip, making a fold line about a third of the way down the object.

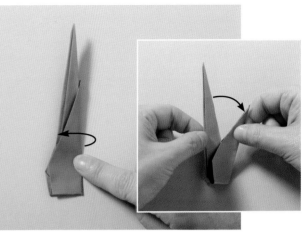

9 Fold the paper in half lengthwise from right to left, then gently pull the two tips apart and press the new fold line flat.

10 Carefully stick the longer point into the hole cut at the base of the tulip flower.

Hako
Gift Box

Giving a gift can be just as pleasurable for the giver as the recipient, especially if the gift box has been handmade. This gift box has a lid that looks like a ribbon bow. It is surprisingly easy to make and looks so fantastic you can even use it as a gift itself.

You will need:
2 sheets of 6in (15cm) *origami* paper (if you are using coloring paper, color it in before you start folding)

Difficulty rating: ✳ ✳ ✳

1 With the colored side down, fold the paper in half from corner to corner both ways, opening out each time, then fold the corners in so that they meet at the center point.

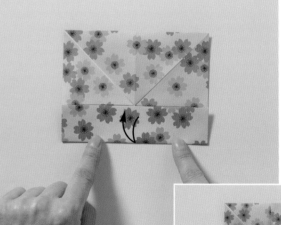

2 Fold the bottom edge so that it sits across the center of the paper and make a crease. Open out and repeat at the top and on both sides of the paper.

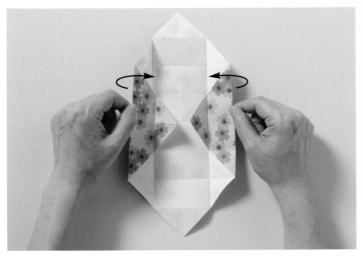

3 Open out the paper until just the sides are folded in.

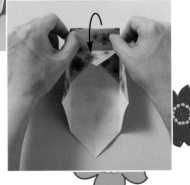

4 Lift the sides to the vertical and fold forward the far point, reversing the direction of some of the creases, so that it forms the end of the box. Fold the tip forward over the edges and flatten it inside the box.

5 Repeat at the other end of the object to make the final side of the box and carefully ensure all the corners sit firmly together.

6 To form the lid, take the second sheet of paper and, with the colored side up, fold it in half from side to side both ways, opening out each time, then turn the paper over and fold in half from corner to corner both ways, again opening out each time. Pick up the sheet and fold it into a square using the creases just made.

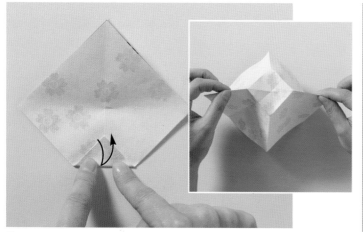

7 Ensuring the folded diagonal edges are at the bottom, fold the bottom point halfway up to the center and make a crease, then lift the paper off the table and open it out, reconfirming the creases toward the edges but leaving the central square flat.

8 Press down the center of this square, forming folded edges around it, then let the two sides of the paper concertina together to reform the original square shape, though now with a flat base.

9 Put the paper back on the table with the flat base toward you and fold up the lower diagonal flaps so that the bottom edges meet along the center line. Turn over and repeat on the other side.

10 Lift the paper up and pull apart the outer flaps, flattening the sheet to reveal a small central square.

11 Fold in the side points and place the tips under the edges of the central square.

12 Turn the paper over and open up the diagonal flaps. Fold the bottom point up to the center and reclose the diagonal flaps.

13 Fold up the bottom edge so that the points of the triangles sit on the center line to make a crease. Repeat from the top and on both sides.

14 Open up the sides and release the top and bottom flaps from beneath the diagonal flaps, then fold the sides back in.

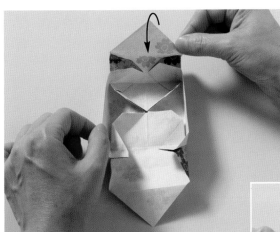

15 Lift the sides to the vertical and fold forward the top tip to form the end of the lid, reversing the creases where necessary. Fold the tip over the newly made edge and tuck it inside the original diagonal folds to keep it in place. Repeat at the other end to finish.

Bara Rose

I made a simple rose using three sheets of red paper, but you can pick any patterns you want, just trim them down to the required sizes. Of all the various ways of making roses with *origami* I recommend this one because it is not difficult and looks beautiful in any color.

You will need:
3 sheets of 6in (15cm) *origami* paper
(if you are using coloring paper, color
it in before you start folding)
Cutting mat, craft knife, and metal rule

Difficulty rating: ✳ ✳ ✳

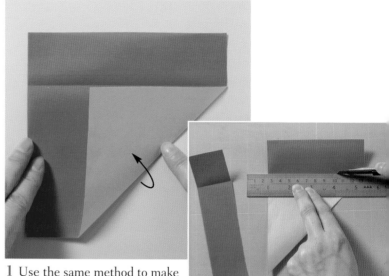

1 Use the same method to make three boxes of different sizes, using 6in- (15cm-), 4in- (11cm-), and 2in- (5cm-) square pieces of paper. To size the smaller sheets, take a piece of *origami* paper and measure 4in (11cm) or 2in (5cm) up one side and fold over one corner to reach the crease. Use a craft knife to cut around the folded corner.

2 Take the largest sheet and with the color side facing up fold from corner to corner and open out. Repeat on the other corner so you have two diagonal creases. Fold the top and bottom edges by eye so that the paper is in thirds and make creases. Open out and fold in the sides. This time use the point where the diagonal crease crosses the horizontal as the fold mark.

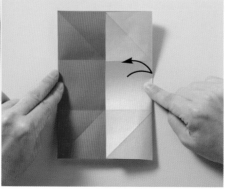

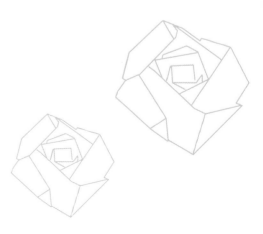

3 Open out the paper and turn it over. Fold the top and bottom edges into the horizontal crease lines, then turn the sides in to meet the vertical creases.

4 Fold over the corners of the last flaps made so that the top and bottom edges run down the sides of the object.

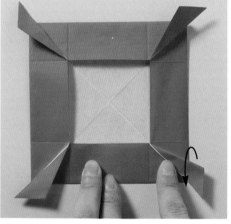

5 Lift each corner and unfold the inner creases, reversing the direction of the folds so that the corners fall outside the edges of the object as triangles. Next turn over the top-right and bottom-left corners across their diagonal creases.

6 Fold over each corner triangle so that the long edges run along the diagonal crease lines.

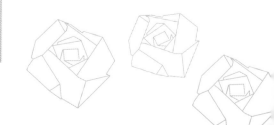

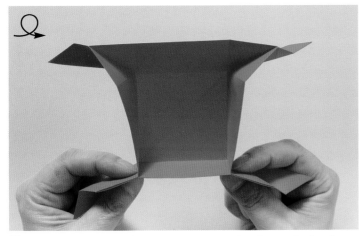

7 Lift up the paper and turn it over. Form the shape of a box by lifting the sides and pressing together the corners.

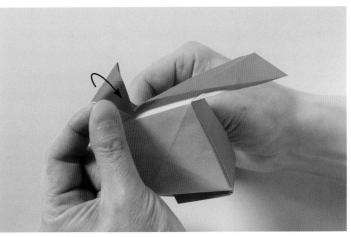

8 Carefully tuck the corner ends under the edge of paper, using the existing diagonal crease lines to hold them in place.

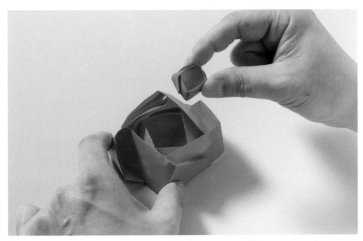

9 Repeat the entire process with the two smaller pieces of paper, then place them inside each other to form the flower.

Beniire Envelope

A traditional *origami* model, an envelope has been long used as a container for small treats like candy or chocolate. It is easy to make—I used two pieces of *origami* paper to show color on both sides, but a single piece would work just as well.

You will need:
2 sheets of 6in (15cm) *origami* paper (if you are using coloring paper, color it in before you start folding)
Paper glue

Difficulty rating: ✳ ✳ ✳

1 Use the paper glue to stick the two pieces of paper together with the colored sides facing outward.

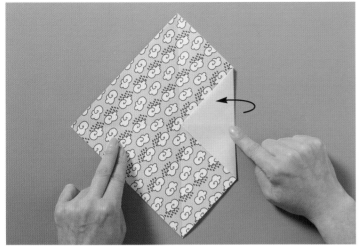

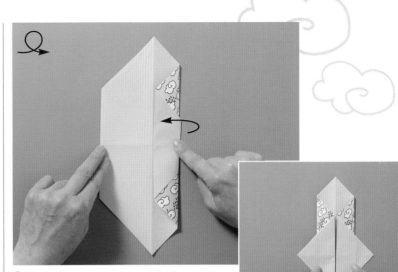

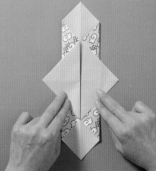

2 Fold the paper in half from corner to corner and open out, then fold in the side points to the crease just made.

3 Turn the paper over and fold the side edges to the central crease, allowing the flaps of paper on each side to be released.

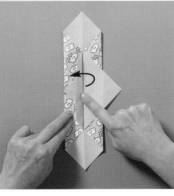

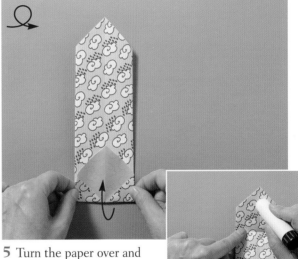

4 Refold each side so that the end point sits on the edges of the paper, then fold back the inner edge of each flap so that they now run down the middle of the object.

5 Turn the paper over and fold in the top and bottom points so that they meet in the middle and hold these last flaps in place by sticking them down with paper glue.

Saifu Card Holder

I made a card holder using a 6in (15cm) square piece of paper, but if you use a piece which is about 12in (30cm) square, you can make a wallet. Using only basic folds, this project is suitable for people who are trying *origami* for the first time.

You will need:

1 sheet of 6in (15cm) *origami* paper (if you are using coloring paper, color it in before you start folding)

Difficulty rating: ✳ ✳ ✳

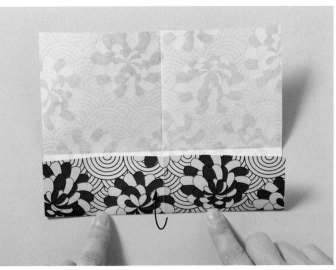

1 With the colored side down, fold the paper in half from side to side, opening out each time, then fold the top and bottom edges in to meet along the central crease.

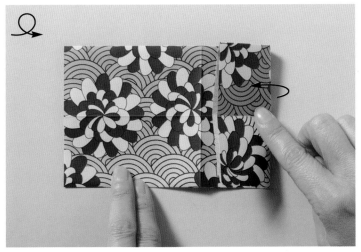

2 Turn the paper over and fold in the sides so that they also meet in the center.

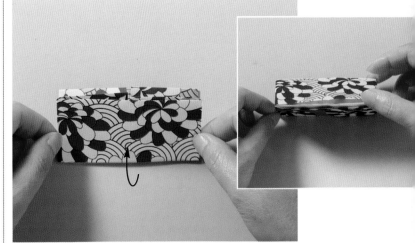

3 Fold the bottom up to the top, then lift the paper and stand it up on the table to allow a card to be slipped into the top.

Kabekazari
Heart Wreath

Use a heart decoration to express feelings of affection. Folding this heart in *origami* is simple, so make a collection of them and have fun creating a wreath or wall decoration. It is easy to make so is one of the items you will always remember.

You will need:
1 sheet of 6in (15cm) *origami* paper (if you are using coloring paper, color it in before you start folding)
Cutting mat, craft knife, and metal rule
Length of cotton

Difficulty rating: ✱ ✱ ✱

1 Cut the sheet of paper into quarters using a craft knife and metal rule. Take the first piece of paper and, with colored side down, fold it in half from side to side both ways, opening out each time, then fold up the bottom edge to the central crease.

2 Turn the paper over and fold up both halves of the bottom edge so that they meet along the central crease.

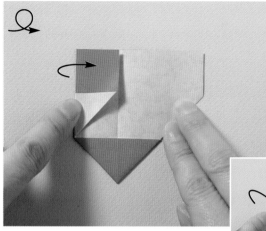

3 Turn the paper over again and fold in the sides so that they meet along the central crease, then turn over the top corners to the central crease to make diagonal folds.

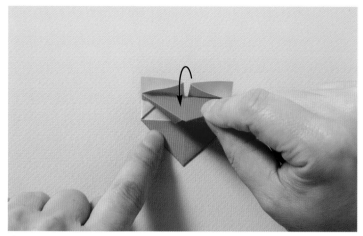

4 Turn down the top point to the bottom, revealing the flaps behind, making a new horizontal crease.

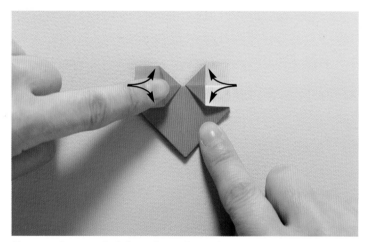

5 Press the revealed flaps down flat to form colored triangles pointing toward each other.

6 Carefully tuck the upper flap inside the lower flap and press flat.

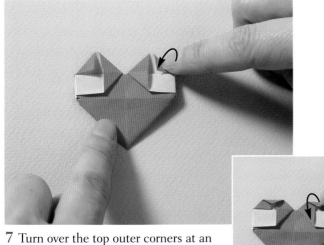

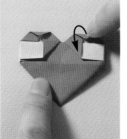

7 Turn over the top outer corners at an angle to make new diagonal creases, then fold over the newly formed top points to make short horizontal edges.

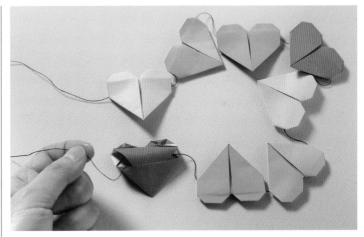

8 When you have made all the hearts, thread them onto a piece of cotton, slightly releasing the tucked-in flap to make it easier.

CHAPTER 2
HAPPINESS
& LAUGHTER

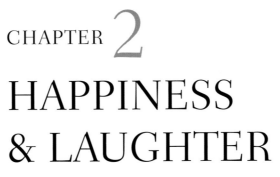

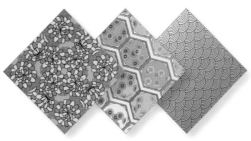

Komonozara Trinkets Tray

This box is a good size for storing small accessories. It is also ideal for chocolate balls and candies, so you could make one for every guest at a children's party. Made in the same way as the famous *origami* "chatter box," it is easy to make even for children and the elderly.

You will need:
2 sheets of 6in (15cm) *origami* paper (if you are using coloring paper, color it in before you start folding)
Paper glue

Difficulty rating: ✳ ✳ ✳

1 Start by sticking together the two pieces of *origami* paper with glue with the colored sides facing outward.

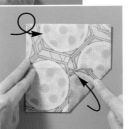

2 Fold the sheets in half from corner to corner both ways, opening out each time, then fold the corners into the center. Turn the paper over and fold the corners into the center again.

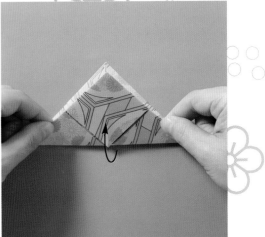

3 Fold the paper in half from bottom to top.

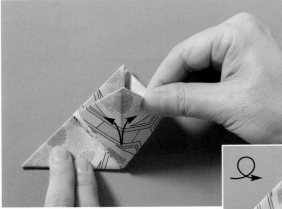

4 Lift the right-hand point and turn it up to the top of the paper, opening up the flap and refolding into a diamond shape. Turn the paper over and repeat.

5 Gently pull apart the outer flaps so that the tray forms its shape and stands up.

Hina-ningyo Origami Doll

Hina-ningyo are made during the *Hinamatsuri*, or doll festival, which celebrates the happiness and healthy growth of girls. Dressed in the costume of Heian-period nobles they have an elegance which is different to the modern kimono style.

You will need:

1 sheet of 6in (15cm) *origami* paper (if you are using coloring paper, color it in before you start folding)
Scissors

Difficulty rating: ✳ ✳ ✳

1 With the colored side down, fold a single sheet in half from corner to corner both ways, opening out the first time. Use a pair of scissors to cut a small slice in the paper at an angle down to the crease line. Open up the paper and refold it in the other direction.

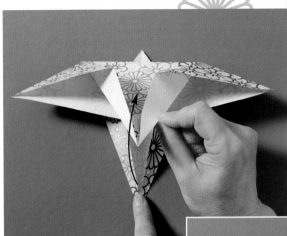

2 Turn up the diagonal edges so that they meet along the center line, then turn the top points down and to the side, making new horizontal edges.

3 Carefully open up the object and lift out the upper sheet of paper. Fold the released point back on itself and tuck it inside.

4 Turn the outer points down toward the bottom of the paper so that the diagonal edges meet along the center line. Fold the same points back out, making new crease lines between the object's new outer points and the top of each flap's vertical edge.

5 Finish by turning the object over and folding up the bottom point which will form a stand for the object when released.

Hashi-bukuro Chopstick Wrapper

When people in Japan give parties for their friends and families they welcome their guests by creating beautiful chopstick wrappers. Decorate the dining table at your own sushi party with such handmade *origami* wrappers.

You will need:
1 sheet of 6x8½in (15x21cm) *origami* paper (if you are using coloring paper, color it in before you start folding)

Difficulty rating: ✳ ✳ ✳

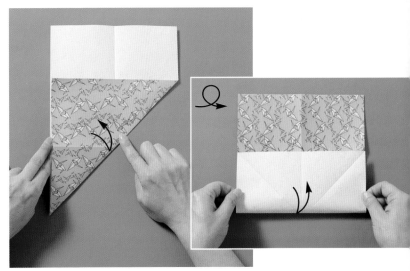

1 With the colored side down, fold the paper in half lengthwise and across its width, opening out each time, then fold the bottom corners across to the other side to make creases. Turn the paper over and fold up the bottom edge, making a new crease line through the point the diagonal creases cross each other.

2 Turn the paper back over and form the bottom into a triangle using the creases made in the first step.

3 Fold in the upper flap from each side so that the diagonal edges meet along the center line, then turn in the newly formed upper diagonal edges so that they also meet along the center line, forming new creases.

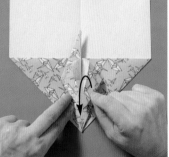

4 Completely open out the right-hand side of the shape made in the center of the object and refold the paper flat into a diamond shape. Pull the top point down to the bottom, reversing the direction of the crease lines where necessary.

5 Fold the upper flap over from the left to the right, then repeat the previous step on the remaining tall flap, finishing by folding the newly formed upper flap on the right over to the left.

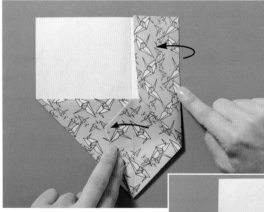

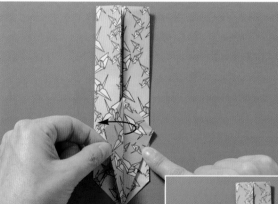

6 Fold over the small flaps in the center of the paper from the right to the left, then fold the right-hand side in so that the edge runs down the center line. Fold the right-hand edge to the center again, then fold all the central flaps over to the right and repeat on the left-hand side.

7 Fold the topmost central flap back over to the left, then lift up the bottom point and fold it upward to form a diamond shape.

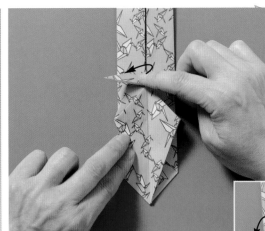

8 Turn the topmost flap on the right over to the left so that it closes up the tall diamond and sits on top of it.

9 Turn over the top of the tall flap at an angle, then carefully open up the flap and refold the tip inside, reversing the direction of the creases where necessary. Next fold over the upper central flap from the right to the left.

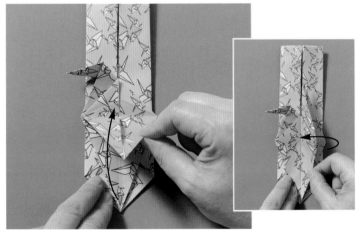

10 Turn up the bottom point to form a diamond, then close the flap by turning it back to the right.

11 To finish, turn over the top of the main left-hand flap at an angle to show where the chopsticks should be placed.

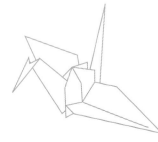

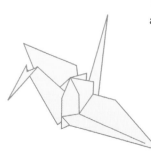

Kashizara Party Tray

This *origami* tray is easy to make so experiment using various sized papers. Alternatively, use a water-proof cooking or parchment paper to make a platter that can be thrown away with any left-overs, making cleaning up after a party so much easier.

You will need:
1 sheet of 6in (15cm) *origami* paper (if you are using coloring paper, color it in before you start folding)

Difficulty rating: ✳ ✳ ✳

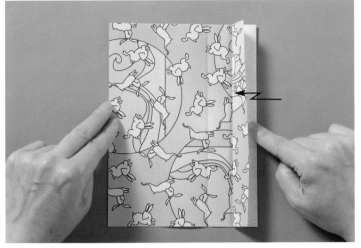

1 With the colored side up, fold the paper in half lengthwise, then fold each side into the middle before folding it back on itself to the new outer edge.

2 Open up the last fold made and turn in the corners of the flaps so that the top and bottom edges meet along the central crease, then turn the corners in again so that the diagonal edges also meet along the central crease. Repeat on the other side.

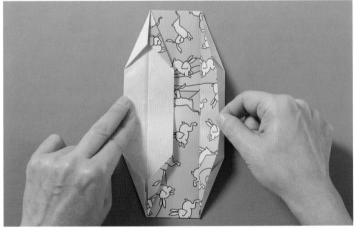

3 Fold the flaps that meet along the central crease over to the outside of the object.

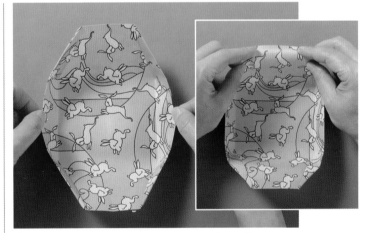

4 Carefully begin to open out the tray by pulling apart the outer edges, ensuring that the corners stay intact. When the shape has begun to appear, roll the ends over to form smooth lips.

Kobako Chocolate box

Filling this small handmade gift box even with just a single piece of chocolate will ensure any treat is especially appreciated. If you use a larger piece of gorgeous paper, you can make it into a wonderful accessory gift box.

You will need:
1 sheet of 6in (15cm) *origami* paper
(if you are using coloring paper, color it in before you start folding)

Difficulty rating: ✳ ✳ ✳

1 With the colored side down, fold the paper in half from corner to corner both ways, opening it out each time, then fold all the corners into the center.

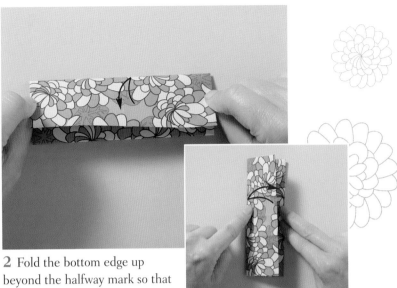
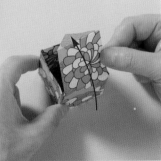

2 Fold the bottom edge up beyond the halfway mark so that when the top is folded down both flaps are of identical length. Only firm up the creases when you are happy this is the case. Open out the sheet and repeat, this time from side to side.

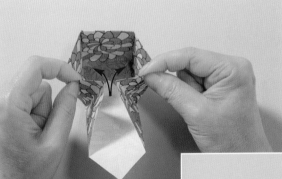

3 Open out the folds just made as well as the top and bottom corners from the middle. Lift up the sides to begin forming the box as well as the far point. Make new creases in the excess paper that is formed at the corners and press them inside the box. Fold the tip over the newly formed top edge and tuck the point into the base of the box.

4 Repeat at the bottom end of the object to form the final wall, though this time use the last open point to form the lid of the box.

Kashibachi Sweet Treat Tray

One of the traditional *origami* models handed down from the old days of Japan, you may feel unsure about it during the first half of the steps because it is inside out. But don't worry because in the end it turns out to be a wonderful candy tray.

You will need:

1 sheet of 6in (15cm) *origami* paper (if you are using coloring paper, color it in before you start folding)

Difficulty rating: ✻ ✻ ✳

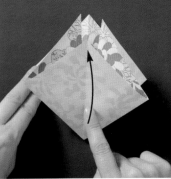

1 With the colored side down, fold the paper in half from corner to corner both ways, opening it out each time, then turn it over and fold it from side to side both ways, again opening it out each time. Use these creases to form the paper into a diamond shape with the creased edges nearest you.

2 Turn the upper flap down from top to bottom, then turn the paper over and repeat on the other side.

3 Turn the upper flap on the left-hand side over to the right, then turn both diagonal edges in to meet each other at the center line. Turn over and repeat.

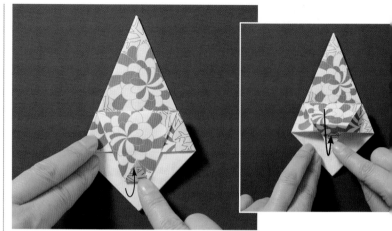

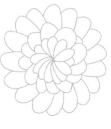

4 Turn the top point of the upper flap down so that it sits on the bottom point and make a new horizontal crease.

5 Turn up the bottom point, then fold the whole flap underneath the horizontal edge of paper, tucking it out of sight. Turn over and repeat on the other side

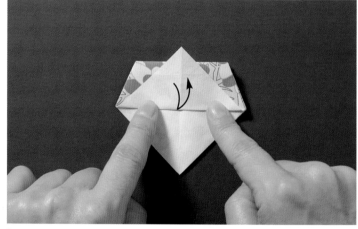

6 Fold the upper flap on the left-hand side over to the right, then turn the paper over and repeat on the other side.

7 Fold up the upper flap from the bottom, making a new crease between the widest points of the paper.

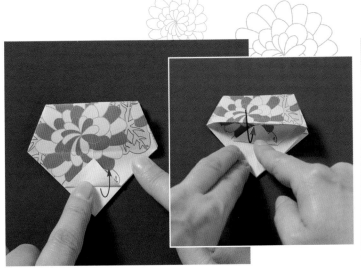

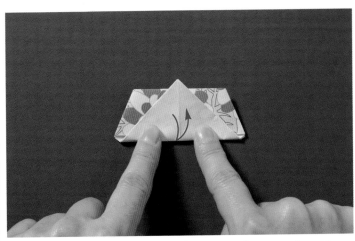

8 Return the flap to its starting point and turn up the bottom point, then fold the end up behind itself, using the crease made in the previous step. Turn the paper over and repeat.

9 Fold up the bottom point to make a crease between the widest points of the object and release.

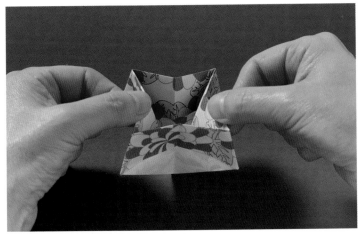

10 Carefully pull apart the sides of the model to form the shape of the tray while ensuring that the floor is flat and even.

Kashibachi Sweet Treat Tray 71

Kidoairaku
Funny Puppet

The Japanese have a proverb, *Warau kado niwa fuku kitaru*—good luck comes to a house with lots of laughter—and the joy created by this *origami* model will ease your body and mind.

1 With the colored side down, fold the paper from side to side, then open and repeat in the opposite direction.

You will need:

1 sheet of 6in (15cm) *origami* paper (if you are using coloring paper, color it in before you start folding)
Coloring pens (optional)

Difficulty rating: ✳ ✳ ✳

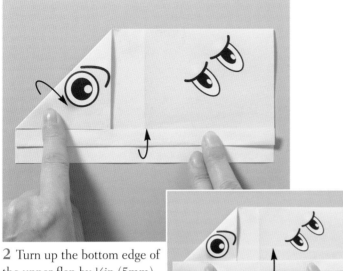

2 Turn up the bottom edge of the upper flap by ¼in (5mm) Next, turn over the top left corner so that the side now runs along the top of the folded flap, before turning the long flap over once more, using the edge of the corner flap as a guide.

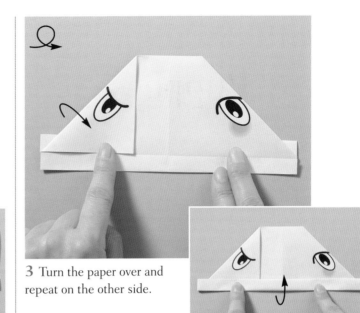

3 Turn the paper over and repeat on the other side.

4 Lift up the paper and open it out, pressing in the top to form the back of the puppet's head. If you are using a plain piece of paper, use coloring pens to draw on some funny cartoon eyes.

Sumo
Sumo Wrestlers

It's fun for two people to play with these *origami* Sumo wrestlers. Make one from patterned paper and create the other wrestler from a sheet of paper you have colored in yourself. Place two of the wrestlers on top of a large upturned paper box and tap the edge of the box in turn with your fingers. The one that falls off first loses the game.

You will need:
2 sheets of 6in (15cm) *origami* paper (if you are using coloring paper, color it in before you start folding)

Difficulty rating: ✳ ✳ ✳

1 With the colored side down, fold the paper in half from corner to corner both ways and from side to side both ways, opening it out each time, then fold the corners into the center before folding them in one more time.

2 Turn the paper over and fold in the upper diagonal edges so that they meet along the center line, allowing the pointed flaps to be released from behind the object.

3 Turn down the top of the diamond shape created using the side points as the fold line, again releasing the tip from behind.

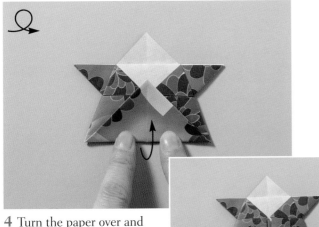

4 Turn the paper over and fold up the bottom point, this time using the lower side points as the fold line, then turn both diagonal edges of the triangle just made down to the bottom horizontal edge to make creases.

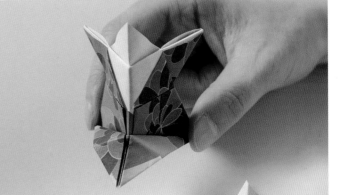

5 Lift the paper off the table and press the sides together to force out the base so that the Sumo wrestler can stand up.

Kemari Origami Ball

This *kemari* ball consists of six units of the traditional *origami* medal stuck together. It was first created as an *origami* model but is now also used as a decoration at celebrations and is often found at children's parties in Western countries.

You will need:
2 sheets of 6in (15cm) *origami* paper (if you are using coloring paper, color it in before you start folding)
Scissors
Paper glue

Difficulty rating: ✳ ✳ ✳

1 Cut both pieces of paper into quarters. Take the first and, colored side up, fold it in half from side to side both ways, opening it out each time. Turn it over and fold it in half from corner to corner both ways, again opening it out each time. Fold the bottom and top edges into the center to make creases.

2 With the paper open again fold the sides into the center to make creases and open out.

3 Turn the paper over and fold in all the corners to the center to make creases. Open out.

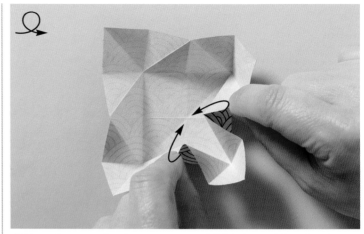

4 Turn the paper back over again and fold the middle of each side over to the middle of the paper. This will allow you to fold a diamond shape at each corner.

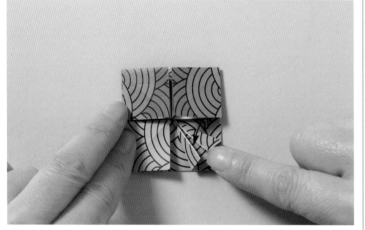

5 Fold over the two inner edges of each corner diamond so that they meet along the center line of the respective diamond.

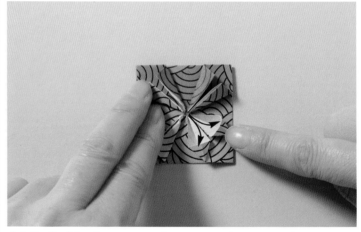

6 Lift all of the flaps just made, opening them out and pressing them flat.

7 To finish, turn the paper over and fold in the corners to create an octagon.

8 Repeat on the seven other pieces of paper, then use the paper glue on the folded corners to stick them together to create a ball.

Kaeru Frog

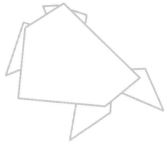

This playful *origami* frog will hop when you press on its back. It requires a little bit of effort to make because you have to fold it many times, but using thinner papers makes it easier. Watching it bounce around will bring a lot of laughter.

You will need:
1 sheet of 6in (15cm) *origami* paper (if you are using coloring paper, color it in before you start folding)

Difficulty rating: ✳ ✳ ✳

1 With the colored side down, fold the paper from top to bottom and open, then from side to side. Without opening it again, fold down the top edge to the middle to make a crease and release.

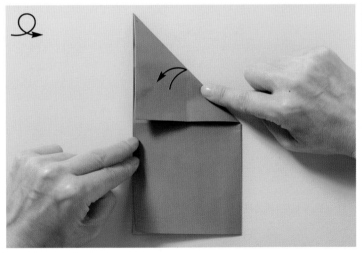

2 Turn the paper over and fold the top corners over to the opposite edges and make diagonal creases.

3 Fold over the top edge to the middle, pressing the sides underneath to form a triangle.

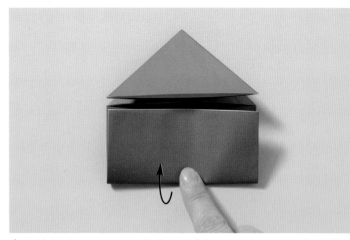

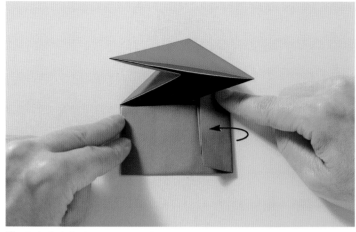

4 Fold the bottom up to the base of the triangle just made and press a firm crease.

5 Slightly lift the triangle of paper and fold the sides in so that they meet along the center line underneath the replaced triangle.

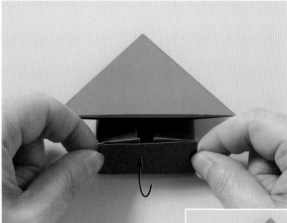

6 Fold the bottom edge up to the base of the triangle again and make another crease, then fold the top corners of the flaps just made over to the bottom edge to make diagonal crease lines.

7 Open up the flaps made in the previous step and pull out the inner edges of paper, refolding them out to the sides of the object. Next fold them both down to the bottom of the object.

8 Fold up the tips of the main triangle at an angle so that the tips break over the triangle's diagonal edges.

9 Fold the bottom points in half so that the long edges run along each flap's diagonal crease line.

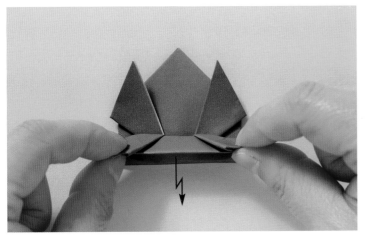

10 To finish, fold up the bottom half of the paper across the middle of the model and turn back the bottom edge to form the back legs of the frog.

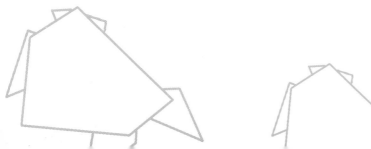

Kingyo
Goldfish

This model is also called "balloon goldfish" as it is based on the traditional *origami* balloon model. You can put paper clips on the tips of the goldfish and play a fishing game—everyone can have some fun, regardless of age.

You will need:

1 sheet of 6in (15cm) *origami* paper (if you are using coloring paper, color it in before you start folding)
Pencil, pen, or other pointed object

Difficulty rating: ❃ ❃ ❃

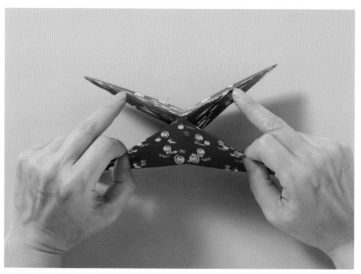

1 With the colored side down, fold the paper in half from corner to corner both ways, opening out each time, then turn it over and fold it in half from side to side both ways, again opening out each time. Turn it back over and form the paper into a triangle using the creases just made.

2 Fold the outer points of each upper flap up to the top point.

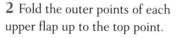

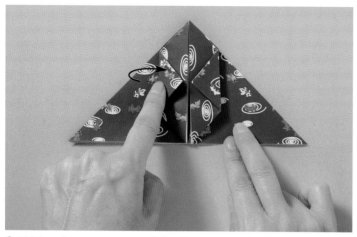 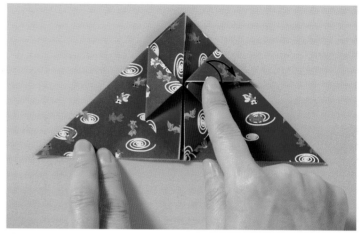

3 Fold in the outer points of the flaps just made to meet each other on the center line.

4 Turn over the top points of the same flaps at an angle to make diagonal creases, using the edges of paper as the fold line.

5 Release the flaps just made and turn down the top point on each side so that the diagonal edge also runs along the diagonal crease line. Now lift the central flap and open up the pocket to allow the upper folded flap to be tucked inside.

6 Turn the paper over and fold over the side points so that the diagonal edges meet along the central crease.

7 Turn just the left-hand flap out to the side of the object, forming a horizontal top edge.

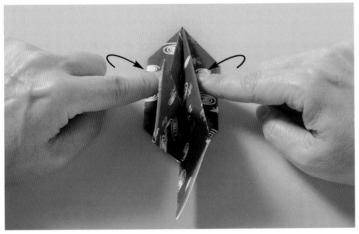

8 Lift the two flaps together.

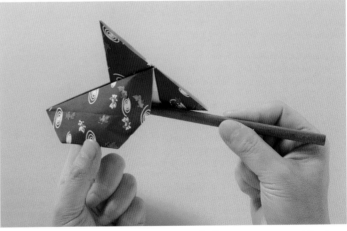

9 Pick up the model and use a pointed object to press inside the object and form the shape of the goldfish's body.

CHAPTER 3

BELIEF &
WILLINGNESS

Ki Fir Tree

Shinrin-yoku, literally meaning "forest bathing," is good for body relaxation. You can create the impression of a little forest by placing these pretty *origami* trees in a corner of your room. Spray on some tree-scented aroma oil, and help relax your body and mind.

You will need:
1 sheet of 6in (15cm) *origami* paper (if you are using coloring paper, color it in before you start folding)
Scissors

Difficulty rating: ✳ ✳ ✳

1 With the colored side down, fold the paper in half from side to side both ways, opening out each time, then turn the paper over and fold from corner to corner both ways, again opening out each time. Lifting the paper up, fold it into a diamond shape using the creases just made.

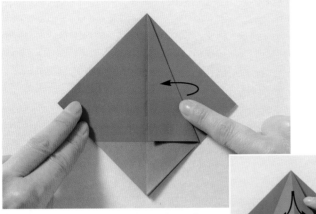

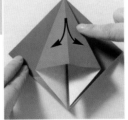

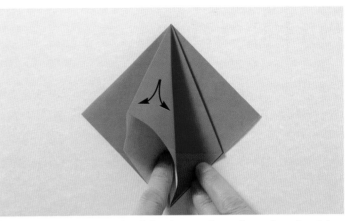

2 Fold in the upper flap from the right-hand side so that the diagonal edge runs down the central crease, then lift and open the flap, refolding it flat into a diamond shape.

3 Turn the left-hand side of the diamond just formed to the right, then fold the left-hand flap into the center before opening it again and refolding it flat into a diamond. Turn the paper over and repeat Steps 2 and 3 on the other side.

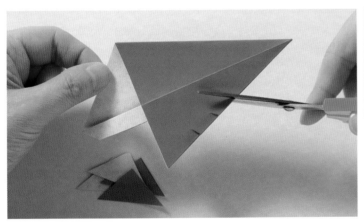

4 Use the scissors to cut approximately ¾in (2cm) into the paper along the line where the edge of the green paper meets the white paper. Make a second cut upward to form one side of the trunk. Make short angled snips down one side of the long green edges. Repeat these cuts to the trunk and the green edge on the other side of the model. Cut off the bottom point of the trunk to form a straight edge for the tree to stand on.

5 Open out the flaps and turn over the edges below each slice to give the impression of a fir tree.

Fune Boat

You can have a fantastic time making this boat while imagining enjoying a relaxing time on a tranquil lake. It is easy to create using a rectangular piece of paper and you can also use it as a boat-shaped tray.

You will need:
1 sheet of 6x8½in (15x21cm) *origami* paper (if you are using coloring paper, color it in before you start folding)

Difficulty rating: ✳ ✳ ✳

1 With the colored side up, fold the paper in half lengthwise and open out. Then fold in half widthwise before turning over the top corners with a folded edge so that their top edges run down the central crease. Next fold up the upper flap at the bottom so that it meets the bottom of the flaps just made.

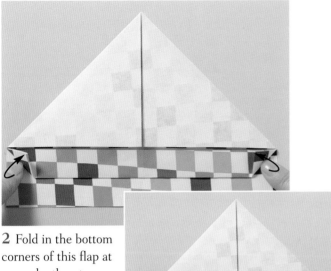

2 Fold in the bottom corners of this flap at an angle, then turn the whole flap up and over the edges of the triangular flaps.

3 Turn the paper over and fold up the bottom edge in the same way, then open up the model and push the right-hand point over to sit on top of the left-hand point, forming a square shape.

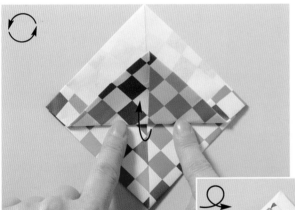

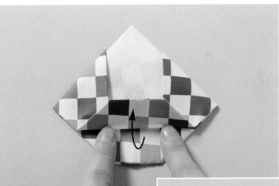

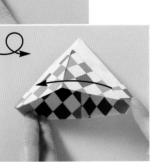

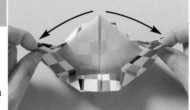

4 Spin the paper to a diamond shape and turn up the bottom point, making a crease ½in (1cm) below the central horizontal line. Turn over and repeat, then fold the right-hand point over to the left.

5 Fold up the bottom edge on both sides and then pull the two flaps surrounding the model's diagonal edges to form the shape of the boat.

Kimono Kimono

The *kimono* is well-known as traditional Japanese clothing but it was only between the late 16th and 18th centuries that the shape developed into the one we know today. Use this *origami* as a message card, writing your message on the back of the beautifully patterned paper.

You will need:
1 sheet of 6in (15cm) *origami* paper (if you are using coloring paper, color it in before you start folding)
Scissors

Difficulty rating: ✳ ✳ ✳

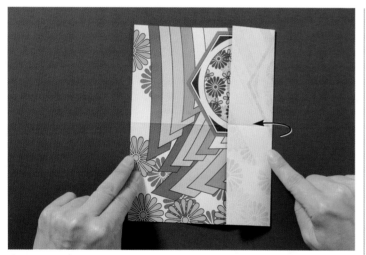

1 With the colored side down, fold the paper in half both ways, opening out each time, then turn it over and fold both edges into the center.

2 Turn the paper over and fold the edges into the center again, this time allowing the flaps to be released from underneath.

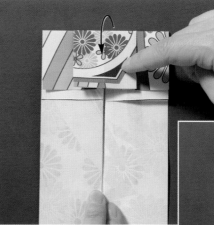

3 Carefully use the scissors to cut along the horizontal crease lines on the upper flaps right into the middle of the paper.

4 Fold the top of the paper over to within ¼in (5mm) of the cut lines, then turn the edge back to the top, ensuring that it ends up ¼in (5mm) over the top edge of the paper.

5 Fold back each side of the upper flap, reforming the central section into triangles, then turn over the outer corners of the central flap.

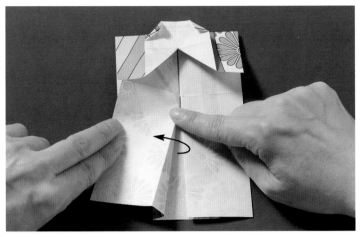

6 Refold the two main flaps at an angle so that the top edge sits slightly above the cut line.

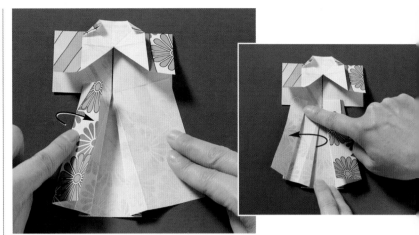

7 Fold these flaps in half, then turn the edge back again so that it sits outside the flap's folded edge.

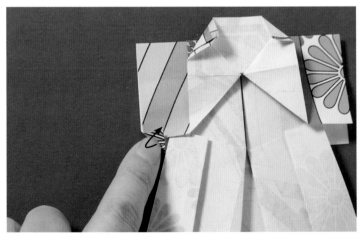

8 Finish by turning up the bottom corners of the lower central flaps so that they hold the upper flaps in place.

Fukigoma Spheres

The *fukigoma* spins when you gently hold the top and bottom with your fingers and blow on it. Created from six easy-to-make units, when you join them together, make sure to hold them tight so they don't separate from each other.

You will need:
2 sheets of 6in (15cm) *origami* paper (if you are using coloring paper, color it in before you start folding)

Difficulty rating: ✳ ✳ ✳

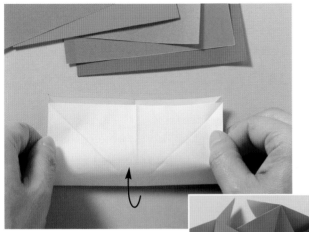

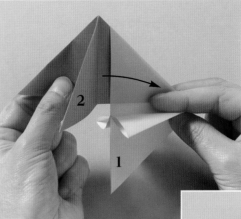

1 Cut the two pieces of origami provided into quarters and take six of the pieces to make this project. Alternatively, use six sheets of different colored paper. With the first sheet colored side down, fold it in half from corner to corner both ways, opening out each time, then turn it over and fold in half from side to side both ways, again opening out each time. Lift the paper off the table and use the creases to fold the sheet into a triangle shape. Repeat on all the other pieces of paper.

2 Holding one sheet with its open edges to the left, slide one arm of the second sheet into the top of the first until it fits snugly. Holding them together, slide the third sheet over the opposite arm of the second sheet, as shown.

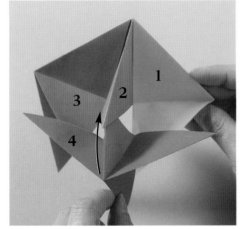

3 Holding all three in place, fit the fourth sheet around points of the first and third sheets while sliding a third point inside a point of the second sheet.

4 Spin the model around in your hands and repeat the last step with the fifth sheet of paper.

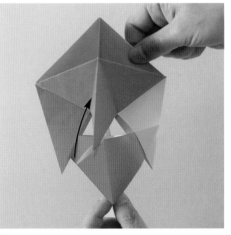

5 Fit the last sheet around the four remaining points of paper, inside two and around the other two. If the cube feels loose, check that only two points for each sheet are visible and adjust accordingly.

Haori Kimono Coat

This model is a coat that is worn over a *kimono*.
It is what a cardigan or jacket is to normal clothes.
However, a black *haori* embroidered with a family
crest is worn at a wedding ceremony as formal dress
even now.

You will need:
1 sheet of 6in (15cm) *origami* paper
(if you are using coloring paper, color
it in before you start folding)
Craft knife, cutting mat, and metal rule
Paper glue

Difficulty rating: ✳ ✳ ✳

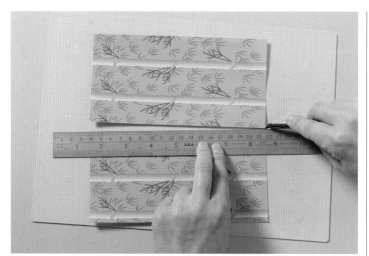

1 Fold the paper in half to make a crease, then open out and use
a craft knife to cut it in half along the crease.

2 Place the pieces of paper end to end and overlapping each
other. Use paper glue to stick them together, making sure that
they are exactly in line with each other.

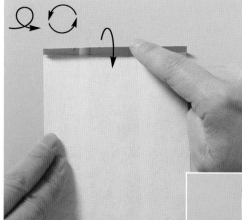

3 Turn the paper over and spin it through 90°, then turn the top edge over by ¼in (5mm). Fold the paper in half widthwise and press a crease down just the top 1in (2.5cm) of paper.

4 Open out, turn over, and fold the top corners over so that their edges meet along the short central crease just made.

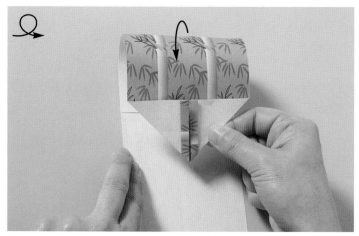

5 Turn the paper over and fold down the top edge so that the ends of each vertical edge sit on the paper join.

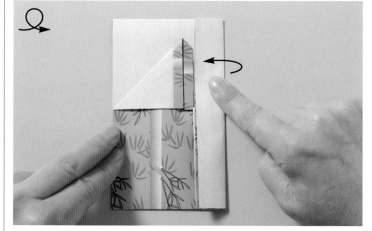

6 Turn the paper over and fold it down from top to bottom, then fold in the sides so that they meet the folds made in Step 3.

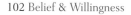

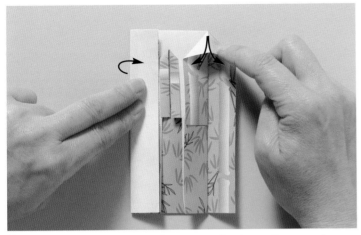

7 Fold back the uppermost sheet on each edge, reforming the top of each side into a triangle.

8 Turn the paper over and fold down the top, making a new crease line between the tops of the paper's vertical edges, leaving a small triangle of paper above the new top edge.

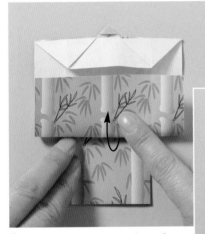

9 Fold the uppermost sheet from the bottom so that it sits along the flap made in the last step, then, to finish, turn up the bottom corners of this new flap to make short diagonal edges.

Tsuriganeso Bluebell

Thousands of bluebell flowers can change a grass field into a blue carpet in spring, letting us know that winter is truly over. Curl the four petals of the *origami* bluebell outward in the last step to make it more like the real bluebell flower.

You will need:

1 sheet of 6in (15cm) *origami* paper (if you are using coloring paper, color it in before you start folding)
Pencil or pen

Difficulty rating: ✳ ✳ ✳

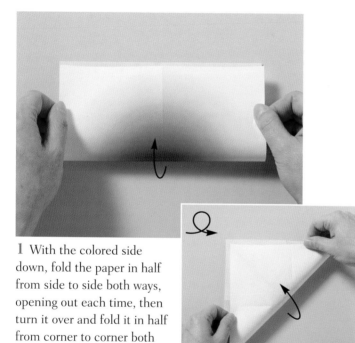

1 With the colored side down, fold the paper in half from side to side both ways, opening out each time, then turn it over and fold it in half from corner to corner both ways, again opening the paper out each time.

2 Lift up the paper and use the creases just made to form the sheet into a diamond shape.

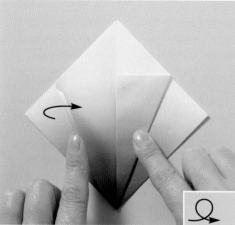

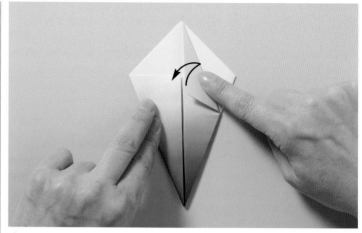

3 With the open edges of the diamond away from you, place the paper back on the table and fold in the lower diagonal edges so that they meet along the central crease. Turn the paper over and then repeat.

4 Fold in the upper diagonal edges to make new creases, checking that they also meet along the central crease.

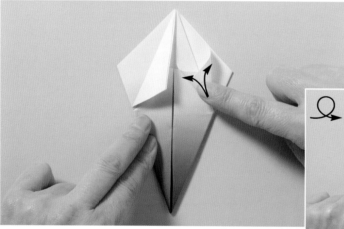

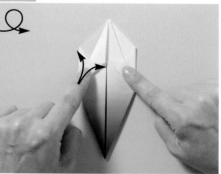

5 Lift the flaps just made and open them out, pressing the two sides flat and forming triangle shapes at the bottom. Turn the paper over and repeat.

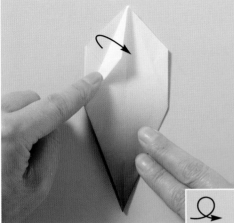

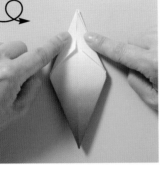

6 Fold the uppermost sheets of both top diagonal edges so that they run down the central crease. Turn over and repeat.

7 Use a pencil or pen to curve the end points of the petals equally.

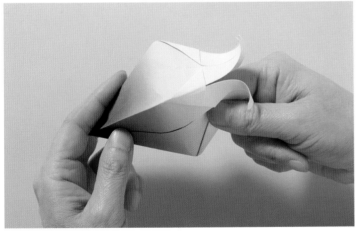

8 Gently use a finger to open out the shape of the flower.

Yaezakura
Springtime Cherry Blossom

The model for this *origami* cherry blossom, *yaezakura*, which has many layers of petals, is one of Japan's best-loved flowers. The arrival of the cherry blossom is essential for recognizing the start of spring and celebrating a new beginning.

You will need:
2 sheets of 6in (15cm) *origami* paper (if you are using coloring paper, color it in before you start folding)
Craft knife, cutting mat, and metal rule
Paper glue

Difficulty rating: ✻ ✻ ✳

1 Use a craft knife with a cutting mat and metal rule to divide both sheets of paper into four quarters each.

2 Fold one quarter in half from corner to corner and open out, then fold the lower edges in so that they meet along the central crease. Turn the top point down over the edges of these flaps to make a crease.

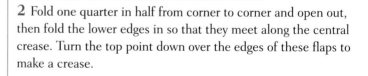

 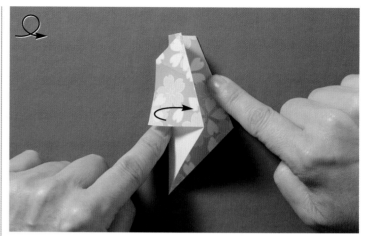

3 Open up the paper and refold the top point, then fold the upper diagonal creases in on top of it so that they meet along the central crease.

4 Turn the paper over and fold it in half.

 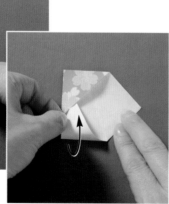 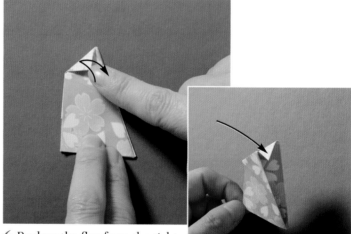

5 Fold the bottom point up across the bottom edges of the flaps to make a crease. Release it and open the top flap to the right, then tuck the bottom point back up and underneath the diagonal edge of paper.

6 Reclose the flap from the right, then turn the top left point of paper over the short diagonal edge next to it to make a crease. Lift the paper, open it up slightly, and refold the corner inside, reversing the direction of the creases where necessary.

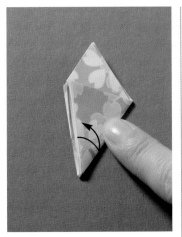

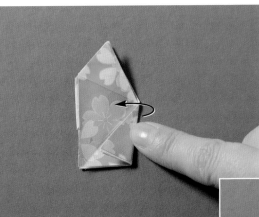

7 Fold up the bottom right corner so that the bottom edge runs up the paper's left-hand side and release to leave a diagonal crease.

8 Turn back the right-hand corner so that the edge of paper now runs along the new crease line, then turn the point back so that the bottom edge runs along the side of the paper.

9 Lift up the paper and open it slightly, refolding the corner inside, once again reversing the direction of the creases where necessary.

10 Repeat the whole process with the other seven quarters and use paper glue to stick them all together to form the cherry blossom flower.

Shumaigiku Anemone

The *shumaigiku* has long been used as base for the traditional *kusudama* sphere. As the flower is easy to make and looks very nice, it can also be made into a brooch using a small piece of paper.

You will need:
1 sheet of 6in (15cm) *origami* paper (if you are using coloring paper, color it in before you start folding)
Craft knife, cutting mat, and metal rule
Paper glue

Difficulty rating: ✳ ✳ ✳

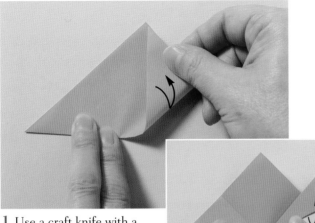

1 Use a craft knife with a cutting mat and metal rule to divide a sheet of paper into four quarters, then fold one of the pieces of paper in half from corner to corner. Next fold the end points up to the top point to make two diagonal creases. Open out and fold up the bottom edges to the creases just made.

2 Turn the paper over. Fold back the tips over the paper's edges to make creases and then release.

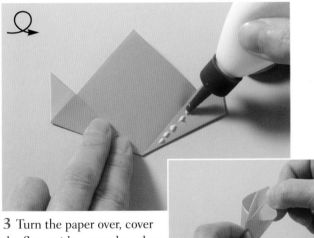

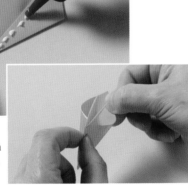

3 Turn the paper over, cover the flaps with paper glue, then press the two flaps together to fix them in place.

4 Repeat the process with the other three quarters of paper and stick the four together with paper glue.

Wakazari Wreath

This *origami* wreath is easy to create so make one from different papers that suit the changing seasons. It will look most exciting when you apply a color gradation or Christmas colors.

You will need:

2 sheets of 6in (15cm) *origami* paper (if you are using coloring paper, color it in before you start folding)
Craft knife, cutting mat, and metal rule

Difficulty rating: ✳ ✳ ✳

1 Use a craft knife with a cutting mat and metal rule to divide both sheets of paper into four quarters each. Take the first piece of paper and fold in half from corner to corner both ways and from side to side both ways, opening it out each time. Next fold in each edge to the center, again opening out each time.

2 Turn the paper over and fold all four corners into the center to make diagonal creases, opening the paper out each time.

3 Turn the paper back over and fold in the middle of each side to the center point of the paper. The corners will fold in on themselves and form diamond shapes.

4 Fold over two corners of each corner diamond so that the points meet along the diamond's central crease to make new creases, then fold them back underneath.

5 Repeat this process on all the other pieces of paper, then carefully slot them together, pushing a corner of one piece down the middle of the preceding piece.

Kusudama Decorative Sphere

This *kusudama* consists of six models called *kikuzara*, or chrysanthemum flower tray, which is one of the traditional *origami* models. It will look best when you use *origami* paper which is colored on both sides. Depending on how many units you combine, you can create spheres of a different size.

You will need:
2 sheets of 6in (15cm) *origami* paper
(if you are using coloring paper, color it in before you start folding)
Craft knife, cutting mat, and metal rule
Paper glue

Difficulty rating: ✳ ✳ ✳

1 Use a craft knife with a cutting mat and metal rule to divide both sheets of paper into four quarters each. Take the first and fold it in half from corner to corner both ways, opening out each time, then fold the corners in to meet at the center.

2 Fold the bottom left corner over to the top right corner, then fold what has become the bottom point across to sit on the right-hand point.

3 Lift this last flap and open it, refolding it to the left in a square.

4 Turn the paper over and lift the left-hand point, opening the flap and refolding it to the right, also in a square.

5 Fold in the two edges from the top right corner so that they meet along the central crease, then turn up the bottom left corner across these creases in order to make a new crease.

6 Release the folds made in the previous step and turn the top right point over to the bottom left, refolding the sides into a long diamond shape.

7 Turn the paper over and repeat on the other side.

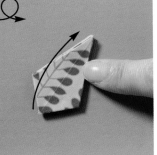

8 Fold the bottom left corner over to the top right, then turn the paper over and repeat on the other side.

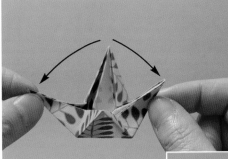

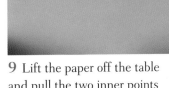

9 Lift the paper off the table and pull the two inner points apart so the outer points flatten into a star shape.

10 Repeat the process with five of the other pieces of paper and then use paper glue on the tips of all the stars to stick them together to make a sphere.

Kabekake Wall Hanging

I joined together versions of the traditional *origami* "medal" into a tapestry that could be placed in a frame and hung on a wall. This one was made sing small pieces of paper so it finished up the size of a greetings card. When attached to a thick piece of paper it will make a card with a unique front.

You will need:
2 sheets of 6in (15cm) *origami* paper (if you are using coloring paper, color it in before you start folding)
Craft knife, cutting mat, and metal rule

Difficulty rating: ✳ ✳ ✳

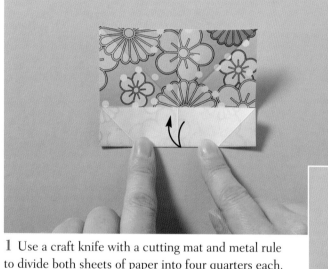

1 Use a craft knife with a cutting mat and metal rule to divide both sheets of paper into four quarters each. Take the first and, with the colored side up, fold it in half from corner to corner both ways and from side to side both ways, opening out each time, then fold all four edges into the center, again opening out each time.

2 Turn the paper over and fold all four corners into the middle to make diagonal creases and then open out.

3 Turn the paper over and fold the middle of each side in to meet at the paper's center point.

4 The creases at the corners will allow them to fold in on themselves to form diamond shapes.

5 Fold the inner corner of each of the corner diamonds over to the outer point.

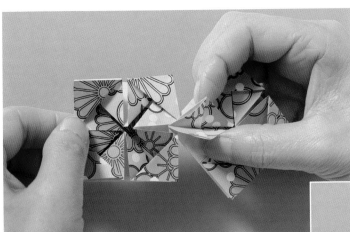

6 Repeat this method on the seven other pieces of paper, then slide the corner of one piece into the middle of one side of another and continue until all of the pieces are joined together.

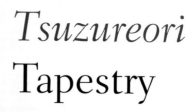

Tsuzureori Tapestry

Using *origami* paper with gradated color, I made this wall hanging by joining the pieces alternately. You can use a variety of *origami* papers and create any number of interesting shapes so try making your own original tapestry.

You will need:
1 sheet of 6in (15cm) *origami* paper (if you are using coloring paper, color it in before you start folding)
Craft knife, cutting mat, and metal rule

Difficulty rating: ✳ ✳ ✳

1 Divide a single sheet of paper into quarters, then follow the previous project instructions to Step 4, forming a square with the corners folded over and sitting on top.

2 Turn one side of the first corner over using the central crease as the fold line.

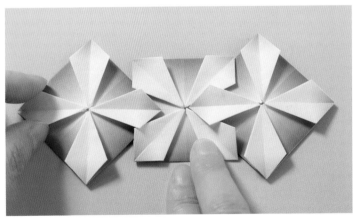

3 Fold the inner edge back to the central crease, then fold the flap back to its original position, so placing the original edge underneath. Repeat all around the paper, then make identical models with the other three quarters of paper.

4 Slip the corner of one piece into the middle of one side of another and repeat until all four of the sheets of paper are joined together.

Useful Information

SUPPLIERS

Origami paper is available at most good paper stores or online. Try typing "origami paper" into an internet search engine to find a whole range of stores, selling a wide variety of paper, who will send packages directly to your home address.
Or please visit first the author's website;
http://www.happyorigamipaper.com

UK
HOBBYCRAFT
www.hobbycraft.co.uk
Stores nationwide
Tel: +44 (0)1202 596100

JP-BOOKS
www.jpbooks.co.uk
24-25 Denman Street,
London
W1D 7HU
Opening Hours:
Mon-Sat: 10:30 - 19:00,
Sun: 11:00 - 17:00
Tel: +44 (0)20 7839 4839
info@jpbooks.co.uk

JAPAN CENTRE
www.japancentre.com
19 Shaftesbury Avenue,
London
W1D 7ED
Opening Hours:
Mon-Sat: 10:00 - 21:00
Sun: 11:00 - 19:00
foodshop@japancentre.com

THE JAPANESE SHOP
(online only)
http://www.thejapaneseshop.co.uk
E mail: info@thejapaneseshop.co.uk

USA
MICHAELS STORES
www.michaels.com
Stores nationwide
Tel: 1-800-MICHAELS
(1-800-642-4235)

Amazon.com
Search for "ORIGAMI PAPER"

eBay USA
Search for "ORIGAMI PAPER"

HAKUBUNDO
www.hakubundo.com

FRANCE
CULTURE JAPON S.A.S.
www.boutiqueculturejapon.fr
Store in Maison du la Culture du Japon
101 Bis.quai Branly 75015,
Pari
Tel: +33 (0)1 45 79 02 00
Fax: +33 (0)1 45 79 02 09
culturejpt@wanadoo.fr

WEBSITES
ORIGAMI USA
http://www.origami-usa.org

BRITISH ORIGAMI SOCIETY
http://www.britishorigami.info

NIPPON ORIGAMI ASSOCIATION
http://www.origami-noa.jp

HIROAKI TAKAI
"ORIGAMI KYOSHITSU"
(Japanese only)

KAMIKEY ORIGAMI
http://playithub.com

ORIGAMI INSTRUCTIONS
http://www.origami-instructions.com

FURTHER READING
The Simple Art of Japanese Papercrafts, Mari Ono (CICO Books)
ORIGAMI for Children, Mari Ono and Roshin Ono (CICO Books)
More ORIGAMI for Children, Mari Ono (CICO Books)
Nihon no Origami Jiten (Dictionary of Japanese origami), Makoto Yamaguchi (Natsume K.K)
Fun with Origami, Kazuo Kobayashi (Kodansha)
Origami Zakka 12kagetsu, Rika Mashisa (Kawade Shobo Shinsha)

Index

Acknowledgments

I've been extremely fortunate that a great many people have helped with the creation of this book—to all of them I say a very big thank you. My editor, Robin Gurdon, has helped me throughout with skill and knowledge and I'm also immensely grateful to the photographer, Geoff Dann, and his assistant, Marcus Harvey.

Getting to work with Robin and Geoff has always been a pleasure. For every one of my books, Robin has always put 100% effort into correcting my English text and explaining clearly how every *origami* step should be done. Similarly, Geoff has also made the work process smoother by giving me simple directions while shooting as well as providing us with great shots for the readers. The completion of the book would not have been possible if these two members were not around, thus the partnership between author, photographer, and editor is always cherished.

The process of designing the paper takes a long time due to the discussion of ideas and the process of marking where the design will go on the paper when finished. This complicated process has always been undertaken by my husband Takumasa, and again without his help the *origami* papers could not have looked this eye catching.

Additional thanks also to Cindy Richards and Pete Jorgensen of CICO Books; Emily Breen for designing; Nel Haynes for styling for this book; and all others who were involved in this publication.